TEACHING

THE

MASTERS

The Instruction Book God
Forgot to Give You

DR JOSEPH CRANE. DD. PHD

ANGEL GATE CREATIONS
501 JOEL LANE
LAKEHILLS. TX 78063

Cover Design and Formatting: Budgetbookdesign.com
Edited by: Diane S. Brown, Dr. Meg Blackburn

First Printing 2003

ISBN 0-9701593-0-7

To my daughter, Gabrayel,
who already knows these teachings.

PREFACE

"**Put down your books for they hold no truth for you. As the sands of the desert have been moved to suit the winds of time, so has the light been darkened by mans ink on the pages.**" These were the very first words spoken to me in the wee hours of the morning by an angelic presence that visited on January 15 of 1995. I was later to find out this angel was the Archangel Michael. Over the past eight years I have continued to have visits from him and many other angels bringing messages of enlightenment and love. He also said to me, "**You will gather seven masters and teach them to teach. They in turn will gather their seven masters and teach them.**" After finding the seven masters he spoke of and teaching them, they went out and gathered their sevens; and their seven would gather theirs.

In my first book *Blessings, Gifts and Deeds* along with my second co-authored book *On the Wings of Heaven,* the story is told of how things unfolded over the three years it took to write them. In the time that passed, more visits brought the most incredible information. The angelic realm is in partnership with human kind to teach us the true love God has for us and they are giving us the power to rise above the dogma that has held us back in our ability to grow along spiritual lines. It is for this reason I have written this book, giving the highest of the spiritual teachings received to date from the angelic realm.

The teachings within are not just for the masters that have been gathered. They are for everyone regardless of what religion is held to be true. As Enoch was given the Book of Knowledge from the Archangel Ratziel, we are given again these self-evident truths for the uplifting of the spirit of all humanity. The chapters in this book hold the teachings that each of us require to move our lives in the direction we truly desire. We no longer have to live out of our circumstances, mishaps and ill fortunes. These are the truths to set us free in the way of the world. They are ancient wisdoms realized by every great master that ever walked the earth.

You hold in your hands the power to live in greatness as a mighty force of nature, if that is what you desire. The choice is yours if you dare to make it.

Bless your Heart,
Dr. Joseph Crane

A WORD FROM THE EDITOR

I am not usually someone who spends a lot of time reading, much less editing, a book such as this. I am, as my family will tell you, the ultimate skeptic. I am that person that telemarketers hate and vacuum cleaner salespeople will refuse to call upon. A middle child between two brothers, I developed a "baloney" detector very early in life and have been using it successfully ever since. So, why am I attaching my name to this work which may be, to the outside observer, a little too "unconventional," for the tastes of your average, extremist skeptic?

During the Christmas of 2001, I was presented with some healing oil to use on my husband's back. Handicapped following a car accident twenty-five years ago, we were willing to try anything short of surgery to ease his constant pain. "Sure," I thought as I rubbed this oil on his back, "this will work because he thinks it will." At that point an idea began to grow in my mind. I would put this stuff to the ultimate test. Alone, after everyone had gone to sleep, I would put it into my bath, as had been recommended for my husband. My legs had ached from painful arthritis and persistent "shin splints" caused by standing and walking for years on concrete floors. If this stuff could ease my pain, then maybe there was something to it.

So, after everyone had slipped into bed and dropped off into dreamland, I drew a hot bath and settled down for a soak. "One drop," I thought. "Hah! Let's give this stuff a fighting chance," I muttered and dropped 10 drops into the water. After a long, tingly bath, I fell into bed. When I woke up, the pain was gone. Not just gone for an hour or a day, but fully gone, as though it had never been there.

When, literally, jumping for joy I thanked those who had given us the oil, they asked me to edit a work that would help continue this work.

How could I refuse?

—Diane S. Brown

TABLE OF CONTENTS

CHAPTER 1

TODAY'S NEW MASTERS

Deep down in everyone's heart is a longing to be great at something and to be recognized by others as the best. This longing is not an accidental feeling nor is it a desire to be better than the rest; this is a connection with and a taste of the mastery that lies in all things. What do I mean by this? Let's explore what a master is thought to be.

The word master has been used in many ways throughout history. A male teacher is said to be a schoolmaster. A master can be a person holding an academic degree, a religious leader, an accomplished crafts person, a person who has accomplished great things, the captain of a ship, a boy or male head of a household or even a person who owns slaves or animals. These examples may be true of the way most of us think of a master. As a part of this definition, we commonly recognize that somewhere along the line, people worked to master a skill or were born the title. This is not to say that they were undeserving of the title due to their efforts or chance of birth; but, because we recognize such a narrow definition of the term "master", most people do not recognize that they are a master.

For many reasons – social, political, economic and religious – similar forms of hierarchy were developed across regions, cultures, and religions. The "rightness" of this model is so deeply ingrained in each of us that it is difficult to think about the word master in any other way. To prove a point, ask yourself if you are a master. If not, what would it take to become one? As you look at the training you would need or the education you must acquire, ask your self "Why?" Are these things that you must have to be called "master"? Do you need the approval of others called "master" to be one your self?

There was one Master who broke this mold. Jesus' life and actions were quite the opposite of the established religious and political laws. He truly understood the four fold natures of mankind those being physical, emotional, mental and spiritual. He was an upstart who came on the scene and began talking of things that were contrary to what had been. He caused a whole new way of thinking to replace centuries of religious and political structures. He did away with an old paradigm and made way for a new way of thinking about the term Master.

This new paradigm is we are, in fact, all masters. To understand this new way of thinking, it is necessary to first understand a new definition of the word, master. Master, for our purposes, will refer to a member of any of the seven different groups of people in society. These groups could be called clans or tribes or referred to as the color associated with each one (the Red people, the Blue people). Because this book is written from a Christian perspective, these groups are called "churches". Every person is a member of one of these seven churches. It is important to note that each of the seven churches has unique attributes and gifts. Each church is marked by a musical note, a color (or vibrational frequency), a stone, and even a day of the week.

These seven churches are spoken of in the *Book of Revelation*. Most people think the *Book of Revelation* is about the end of the world. They become locked into thinking Revelation deals with the anger of God for our sins. When God is seen as a vengeful being, it is natural to interpret the events in the *Book of Revelation* as punishment that will befall the unfaithful. Nothing could be further from the truth. Revelation was given to John that he might share the truth and the love of God with his brothers and sisters. What John received was misunderstood, misinterpreted and written erroneously. The message given to John was never meant to threaten or strike fear in any of God's children. The true message is God's unconditional love for all of us.

After receiving this information from Michael about each church, I decided to try a search on the Internet to find information on each and every church or city. To my surprise, I found out some very unexpected information. First of all there really was a connection between the churches and colors that Alexander Everett spoke of in his book, *"Inward Bound."* The colors of the rainbow could fit in rather nicely with these churches. Secondly, I was surprised to find how well the city and church fit with what Michael was telling me about them.

Below, then, is a discussion of the true meaning of each of the seven churches. In each case, the first information (in bold) was given directly from the angel, Michael, to the author of this work. Some of the more pertinent historical and geographical data is next, followed by a brief explanation of the specific gifts and attributes of the church being discussed.

"To the church of Smyrna, God said to teach illumination of self through faith, and they heard not."

Smyrna is female in the gift of life as a mother is. As in the beginning before birth, a woman knows that there is life. Intuition is the foundation

that gives birth to faith. Listen to that which God is telling you and you will know not the fear of death. John's message to this church is to listen to the truth of God. False teachings will lead you away from your gift and you will know it not. Those that claim to have authority of God, have it not. Let them say what they will, for it is you that will have the victory over the second death.

The first church is Smyrna. This church is female in nature, and as female it is intuitive. The people of this church have a gift for teaching others to see the truth in them selves. The faith they call forth in others opens the door to that of insight. They know things without being told and have faith in what they know. They lead others to a better place in life, from darkness to light - where they go others follow. They are always being enlightened with God's love for them and others.

The trap that is for them is made by them selves. They will speak of them selves as unworthy. They will listen to the lies of others about them and believe it is so. They will lose union with their gift and sleep though they are awake. In this sleep they are truly lost, for they can't lead and they will not follow. For them to awaken they must listen to what God is telling them and know the power they are.

RED or **Smyrna** is synonymous with Myrrh used

as a healing ointment, especially for embalming the dead. Myrrh is made by crushing and **bleeding** this plant. The more the plant is crushed and bruised, the greater the fragrance. The city was built around Mount Pagus. Because of its splendor and its garland of magnificent buildings, the hilltop was known as the crown of Smyrna. All through her long history massacring armies, earthquakes, plagues and fires attempted to destroy the city. Smyrna is the only city of the seven cities that has any of its ancient grandeur remaining. It is now the largest city and commercial center in Asia Minor, with the modern name, Izmir.

The church Smyrna takes the role of leader or a pathfinder. These people become leaders and pathfinders by using their gifts and the attributes of these gifts. The attributes of the gifts of Smyrna are illumination, faith, intuition and the balance between love and wisdom. People of this church are truly ministers of justice and keepers of the peace. They are physical in nature and know the true meaning of oneness. Faith gives them their driving force of courage and heroism. The color of the church Smyrna is red; and, like the color red, people of this church stand out in crowd. The stone that vibrates with their frequency is the ruby. The bloodstone is another red stone for this church but it vibrates with a different frequency. Bloodstone signifies infrared, a color humans cannot see. Only a master who is balanced spiritually and physically can use a bloodstone. The musical note for this church is G, and the day for this church is Sunday.

"To the church of Ephesus, God said teach divine love and grow in spirit, and they heard not."

Ephesus is female in being and teaching. This church is as a mothers love teaching her children of God's love. With knowledge of this divine love, her children will grow in spiritual connection to God. John's message to this church was to put down its obedience to her new husband and return to her children, lest they grow to be unknowing in spirit. Taken away will be their gift if they do not; but they will eat the spiritual food of God if they listen.

The second church is that of Ephesus. This church is female in nature and as female it is a mother to all. This church has been called the church of Mary. Like the mother of Jesus, their gift is the uplifting of others. The men and women of this church are people of divine love. Their joy is giving of them selves for the happiness of others. They can see the divine light that shines in everyone and everything. They speak of it freely, wanting God's children to play and find the joy of life. They will support others in their work and will defend the greatness of those they love.

There is a trap for them in their very nature that they must be watchful of. Their desire to lift every-one and everything up to its true magnificence is the nectar of life for them. They may find them selves as a butterfly fluttering from one flower to the next being lost in the excitement of the flight. As an old bride to a new husband, the fire of the moment burns with passion and the children are forgotten. They forget the gifts they are and look to what they do to make them worthy. This church thinks it has need to suffer and do penance if all does not go well. Their freedom rests in the gifts they are, and only when they see this will they give to them selves. The gift to them selves opens their hearts to the divine love they hold.

ORANGE or **Ephesus** means "desirable". It was considered the most desirable city of the province of Asia Minor. Having one of the best harbors in the world, ships visited from all nations. This made Ephesus one of the main commercial centers of the western coast of Asia. The city was also known as The Light of Asia, and the people promoted many myths and legends of gods and goddesses, making it one of the sacred cities of the pagan world. The temple of Diana, located here, was one of the seven wonders of the ancient world and made the city famous. The city was known for the priests and priestesses dedicated to prostitution in service to the temple. The city met with a sad end as the harbor filled in and the sand took over, turning it into a desert wasteland. This city moved like a butterfly does when the nectar is gone.

Ephesus is the church of the advocator and is truly a defender of divine love. With a motherly love, its people want only the best for others. People of this church are instructors of healthy living and are able to teach ways to experience the fullness of life. They are emotional, generous, forgiving, and embrace duality by being able to see both sides of anything. Orange is the color for this church, and the stones vibrating with their frequency are the orange Sapphire, the orange Calcite or Carnelian. The musical note for this church is E, and the day of the week is Monday.

"To the church of Pergamum, God said to teach consciousness of natural knowing, and they heard not."

Pergamum is male in spirit and knowing of God's love. You hold in your heart the truth and knowing of God's love; you will not be moved. If the teaching of half-truths are told, you will gain that which serves no one in spirit. If you gather that which does nourish the spirit, your deeds will be made open for all to see. Hold true for God will feed the spirit and forgive all that has been done.

Pergamum is the third church. This church is male in nature and seeks truth and knowledge to give to his children. Like a father will find light to guide the way for his children in the darkness, this church is the one that makes the maps. Into uncharted territory he will explore the best paths lest his children should come to harm. Of all the churches, this church will find the truth in the most cunning of lies. The sum of all wisdom is at their beck and call, and that which is true they will find.

The trap for those of this church is lack of faith in them selves. It is their desire to be certain that what they say is true and that will be their undoing. They become internal and lose the reason for their work, and their gift is lost to them. They will give bits and pieces of the truth until not even they can put them together again to make sense. The way out of this trap is for them to give them selves the gift of natural knowing; connect to their own consciousness and reason. That is their gift that will set them free.

YELLOW or **Pergamum** was named for its lofty hills on which the city was built. The name means tower, height, or evaluation and gives one the **idea of exaltation**. It was the exalted city. Pergamum had only one path into the city and was considered an impregnable stronghold. Great philosophers and thinkers such as Homer and Herodotus, studied and wrote there because of its great library, second only to Alexandria.

Pergamum is the church of the higher mind or the intellect. From this church come philosophers, conscious thought, natural knowing and seekers of truth. They are holders of great knowledge and will reason out any questions. People of this church are mental in nature. In their thinking lies divine creativity. Their color is yellow, and the stone vibrating with their frequency is yellow Sapphire, yellow Calcite or yellow Topaz. Their musical note is D, and their day is Tuesday.

"To the church of Sardis, God said to teach awareness and reason, and they heard not."

Sardis is male in thinking, the mental understanding of the love of God. Clearheaded are those in truth, unlike those that seem to be awake but yet they are asleep. Reason is not known to them and all that God has told of his love will pass them by. Those that would stay awake; God will give authority to speak the truth and the false teachings will shatter like clay pots.

Sardis is the fourth church. This church is also male in nature and those of this church are drawn to cure things. That which is bent they will make

straight and that which is broken they will mend. They are truly the healers of the churches in the works they do. Their work consumes them and is nourishment for them.

The trap that they fall into is they begin to feed on the gift they have. They become their task and are lost in the drunkenness of their authority, only to find them selves empty and alone. The path out of this trap is to give from nothing save for the love of God. The power they have comes from God alone and no other can fill it. This is the gift they have and must give to them selves.

GREEN or **Sardis** was the capital city of the kingdom of Lydia and its people were said to have been the inventors of coined money. They were very successful in the fields of commerce and economics. Sardis was inaccessible except by one narrow passage that was steep and easily fortified. This city was also thought to be an impregnable fortress. Being unconcerned about a possible attack, the king thought the wealth was safe, but all was lost. Unlike Smyrna, a city that was dead but thrives today, Sardis' history was just the opposite. Once a prosperous city, it fell but did not recover, and is a dead city today. An interesting footnote, over the years a temple was built in Sardis. It was destroyed and rebuilt many times. This is partly because of the spiritual healing that took place with the people.

Sardis is known as the church of the healers. Those of this church have a willingness to give of them selves to others. They teach awareness and divine wisdom, bringing enlightenment and insight. Their knowledge is mystical and can heal both physical and mechanical. They are at peace in the spiritual sense, in touch with their five senses, and through this combination along with awareness they bring health to all around. Green is the color of their vibrations. The stones equal to this are Emerald, green Kyanite and green Fluorite. The musical note that vibrates to their essence is A, and their day is Wednesday.

"To the church of Philadelphia, God said to open the gates of wisdom, and they heard it not."

Philadelphia is the male seat of passion and the gate of emotions. The key that you hold is that of outgoing love; the gift, the giving. Other emotions that you have would lead you astray if it were not for the love. Hold fast to the love and wisdom, for the other emotions will bow to you. For this, you will be given an understanding of God and all that is of God.

Philadelphia is the fifth church. This church is male in nature with the gift of passionate wisdom. Knowledge is the driving force of this church as a gift to all God's children. Teaching is as the very

air they breathe. These are the ones that hold the keys of wisdom that unlock the gates to let in the light. They are aware of body, mind, emotions and spirit and are in touch with both female and male aspects for them selves. They love all God's children equally, setting none higher or lower than the other.

The trap for those of this church is the loss of any of the four-fold natures given to all human kind. When the balance is gone the giver cannot give and the teacher will not teach wisdom. The escape from this trap lies in the gift of the wisdom and love given back to them selves.

BLUE or **Philadelphia** means brotherly love. It was sometimes called little Athens because of its magnificent buildings and Greek culture. In time Greek was the only language to be spoken there. Philadelphia guarded and commanded an important pass through the mountains and was thus the keeper of the key to the door, or gateway to the east. Through this portal passed information and commerce to and from the east. The city of Philadelphia was in the middle of grape country and it was said to be in the midst of a blue sea of vines. The city Alasehir, as Philadelphia is called today, still continues the tradition of harvesting grapes.

Philadelphia is the church of the teacher. Those of

this church are the keepers to the gates of wisdom. Their personal love is giving to others. They are one with Christ's consciousness and perfectly balanced in the male and female. Of all the churches they are the most balanced in the body, emotions, mind and spirit—the four-fold natures of man. The color vibrating with their essence is blue. The stones of this church are blue Sapphire, blue Aventurine, or Azurite. Their musical note is C, and their day of the week is Thursday.

"To the church of Thyatira, God said to teach love as Jesus did, and they heard not."

Thyatira is male in physical; the action of teaching of the love of God. You are doing the work that God has given you to do. Do not listen to the teachings that call you only to the physical world and of these things. All that is done will be undone, when truth is returned. Guilt will be laid upon those that gathered material things only and it will be laid on them by them selves. To those that kept the balance will carry not or lift upon them selves this burden called guilt. Hold fast and you will be known for loving as God does.

Thyatira is the sixth church. This church is male in nature. The gift of this church is that of a father holding his children in love. The male and female give teachings that are soft and gentle of

27

words. They open their ears and hearts to what the children say. There is no judgment in what they hear, only the love for those in turmoil and how can they be helped. As a father labors with his body to feed his children, so does this church. This church is the master of the song, dance and creates with his hands things of beauty of which lessons are learned.

The trap that this church may fall into is that of the material things. When they go searching for material and physical needs they may lose union with the gift they are to give. The wanting of riches leaves them poor in spirit and in gold. The song they sing is sour, the dance is that of the lame and the creation of their hands is twisted and unkind to the eye. The escape from this trap is to give their gift back to them selves. God will supply all that is needed for the fatherly care of his children.

PURPLE or **Thyatira** was noted for it artisans, trade guilds, and especially for the art of dyeing. The madder root from the region of Thyatira and the water found there were perfect to make a particular color worn by royalty called royal purple. Their other industry was the manufacturing of things made of brass, bronze, and other metals. Thyatira has the fewest archeological remains of any of the ancient cities and is not referenced in old historical records. It was not a fortified city and was destroyed and rebuilt many times. Its name was said to mean "sweet savor of labor".

Thyatira is the church of creation. Those of this church are priests and spiritual teachers in the art of creation. They are ministers of divine love, expressing that love through art, science, and music. Contemplation and sincerity bring forth justice in the work they do. Purple is the color of this church's vibrations. The stones that match these vibrations are Amethyst and Benitoite. The day of this church is Friday and its musical note is F.

"To the church of Laodicea, God said to teach compassion and tolerance, and they heard not."

Laodicea is female with the gift to manage the home. As a woman runs the house, you will lead with understanding for those that know not. You will guide with mercy and tenderness in the words you speak as the woman of God's house. Know that you are loved and stand in the light of God, for true wealth is there. Speak of this love with authority and take your place to one side or the other. Give not your silence to those that would hear. Listen to your heart for God speaks; ignore it not.

The last of the seven churches is Laodicea. This church is female in nature and as female, it is a

mother to all. People of this church have a natural sense of nurturing. This gift is given to both men and women as a path in life and in teachings. They are the ones that care for others as their children. They solve conflicts, being understanding of both sides with compassion; never making one or the other wrong. Tolerance is the teaching they share easily and people listen to them and learn to live and work together. They are merciful to those that have wronged them and do not seek revenge. The tenderness in their hearts lights the world.

There is a trap that those of this church must look for in the work they do. So caring are these persons that they will not teach out of the fear they might hurt another's feelings. When this happens they them selves think they are unworthy to give the gift they were given. They become silent and take no action one-way or the other. They become poor in spirit and forget they are wrapped in God's love. They cannot see the gift they have been given and find no riches in what they do. The way to free them selves of this is to give to them selves the gift that they have been given. When this is done they will be a light to the world.

VIOLET or **Laodicea** was named after the wife of Antiochus to honor her, but she later poisoned her husband. When the city was destroyed in an earthquake the citizens refused help from Rome and rebuilt the city them selves at their own expense. Laodicea was a resort for healing because its waters ran hot and cold. Its lukewarm springs were the most abundant. The eye salve from Laodicea, called collyrium, was sold throughout the known world and was said to give spiritual vision. Laodicea was very much the Paris of its time.

Laodicea is known as the church of the Saints. Those of this church are the most compassionate, tolerant, and tender of all the churches. They show mercy and unconditional love to all. They are truly bringers of light and givers of divine love. They are the joyful ones. In spirit they are confidant, faithful, and bring about completion. Their color is violet, and the stones vibrating at the same frequency are lavender Jade, violet Calcite and Charoite. Their musical note is B, and their day of the week is Saturday.

These seven types of people, the seven churches, are not an accident or random chance. Seven has been identified for centuries as a magical or mystical number. There are seven days to a week and the body rebuilds its self, cell by cell every seven years. In the rainbow there are seven colors. There are seven main notes in a musical scale with the eighth note being the higher note of the next octave.

The religious writings are filled with the number

seven. In Islam there are seven external and internal factors that facilitate performance of prayer, and there are seventy-seven branches of the faith. In Buddhism, there are seven basic elements of life and seven stages of life. In Hinduism and Taoism, there are seven immortal beings. The Jewish people were required to release their debtors of their debts every seven years. The Pharaoh's famous dream regarding famine in Egypt had seven fat cows and seven skinny ones. In the New Testament Christians are told to forgive seven times seventy times. And, of course, the *Book of Revelation* is filled with references to the number seven.

The number seven appears in the legend of Atlantis, also. In the time of Atlantis there was a cataclysm that took place, and Atlantis sank into the ocean in a single day. Imagine the panic that took place, people trying to save whatever they could as it became clear that this great civilization was rapidly coming to an end. There was no way everyone could be saved, and they were left with only one option. Atlantis must be rebuilt somewhere else. Groups of people must be formed that could get the job done. It took seven different types of people to provide the leadership to rebuild a civilization, each person selected for the gifts or talents he or she possessed. The seven were the leader, the advocator, the philosopher, the healer, the teacher, the artist and bearer of light (the person who held the spiritual and political knowledge). According to legend, within these groups were the seeds of all the civilizations that came to be.

In a 21st century model, these seven are the foundation needed to have a successful business. Successful operations will need a red for management and an orange to promote the business. A yellow will best handle research and development while the green is needed to oversee the finances. Blue takes care of educational needs, conducting classes to instruct the public and the employees about the business. The purple would create the advertising and the violet would handle customer service and human resources. The same structure works for any type of community, from the boardroom to producing a television show. Obviously, it is no accident that the number of churches equals seven.

Of which church are you a member? What gifts do you have? Take the time to delve within yourself, and then give your giftedness to the world. As you give, will have an abundant and prosperous life. You will find that when you are contributing out of the giftedness, you will be happier and under much less stress. Like the guy in the old TV show used to say:

"Be what you is,
not what you is not,
cuz folks that what is,
is the happiest lot."
—Rocky and Bullwinkle

CHAPTER 2

MASTERY IN ACTION

This chapter provides the foundation of all the spiritual teachings from the angelic realm. It was taken from my first book titled *Blessings, Gifts and Deeds,* (subtitled, *The Book of Bricks*) originally written to assist Masters in their daily life. As a Master, each of us knows that there are things we should be doing; yet, there is so little written to help us along the way. True, there are great spiritual writings that give lofty ideals about one esoteric concept or another. From reading them we may see things in a different light, but they really don't offer much to help us in taking action. *The Book of Bricks,* on the other hand, gives us practical information that we can act upon, to experience and fully use the mastery in our lives. We don't have to stumble along, taking whatever is served up to us by life. We are no longer victims reacting to what is going on around us. We can become a force of nature contributing to the world around us, making a positive statement and taking a stand about who we are by the actions we take.

The Book of Bricks contains three smaller books. The first is the *Book of Blessings*. When incorporated into our daily lives, we learn to train our emotions and become more loving and kind. As we change, so do those around us. We find ourselves having our emotions under control, and we start to live a more peaceful life.

The second book is the *Book of Gifts*. Working through this book, we educate the mind to accept higher concepts in our thinking. Our minds will become freed of endless mental chatter about nothing and filled with important thoughts. This in turn enhances our entire thinking process so we make fewer mistakes in our actions.

The third is the *Book of Deeds*, which teaches the body to take action out of our spiritual beingness. As humans we have an innate desire to accomplish goals in our lives. When we are unclear or emotionally upset, our ability to accomplish in the physical world is effected. We may find ourselves sitting around waiting for something to change before we are able to get moving and get something done. The *Book of Deeds* contains exercises that will get us participating in life again.

As we become practiced incorporating these into our daily lives, we become a causal agent in our lives and the world around us. We will find ourselves handling things with ease that used to baffle us. Our days will become adventures, rather than drudgery, as we are waking up in the morning ready to fully participate in the business of living. We will find that the mastery we have been searching for is ready to be awakened within us rather than being at the end of a very long quest. These books contain a path that we can follow as the Masters we are. None of this is a have to, nor are we punished for not taking this path. There are many paths a Master can take, this one is offered for its simplicity and the spiritual growth springing from its very core. It is not **the** be all and end all, nor is it **the** truth, the light and the way. It is, however, **a** truth and **a** light and most assuredly it is **a** way.

THE BOOK OF BRICKS

You have all chosen to be flesh and blood, with a time to work out sums. You may have as many lifetimes as you need. Yet there is a point when all must be done. This time is known as the Grand Gathering when God's children will be called home. A quickening has begun at this time before the Gathering, so you may add bricks to your mansion. So long have you been away from your home, that you have forgotten it. You have built a new home out of dust in a faraway land. This house you will not keep, for it is of worldly things. Many of you have labored for worldly things for long years, while setting aside your real reason for coming to earth.

I give this book so you may remember and build your mansions in Paradise. This is not a book of laws you must obey. Nor is it a book by which you may judge your neighbor. There is no punishment if you do not use it to make bricks. You are given this book out of love so you may make the number of bricks you want. Your time is short before the calling. And when you are called, your mansion will be complete. Not one brick will be added or taken away from your labors. That which you have built will be yours for all time. When your mansion is finished you will come home to it. God will furnish it with all the wondrous things your imagination can hold. You will share Paradise with all you have ever loved or were loved by. I tell you now. You must never set this book above one another. You will not hold it as holy or sacred. You will worship it not. It will not be kissed or held with affection in any way.

The Book of Bricks is written in three parts. Each is equal unto the other and none is greater or lesser in value. The first text is of Blessings. This part deals with emotional training. The second is the text of Giving. This part trains the mind. The third text is of Deeds. This part is to train the body. The three stand as separate legs of a tripod. Each is planted firmly on a solid spot. They rise upwards toward a center that holds the platform. On the platform is mounted a transom (the soul) to make sure your direction is straight and level.

THE BOOK OF BLESSINGS

So that this leg may stand on solid ground and your blessings begin, once-blessed are you who take this leg to heart. Some will find it the easiest to set, while others will find it almost impossible. Yet, set it firmly and you will be giving your first blessing to you. Bless my soul, for I am a child of God. Bless my heart for it beats to serve you my God and your children. God has made me perfect, whole and complete for I am in God's own image and likeness. With this knowledge I am all I need to be. I set this leg as the foundation of God's will for me and all others.

The deep feeling of infinite compassion is not just an emotion. This oneness with God sets in motion an uncontrollable desire. Your soul wishes only love and well-being for a person, place or thing. When this happens you make a brick by saying "Bless its heart." There is no blessing so small that it does not make a brick. Saying a blessing only so a brick will be added to your mansion is done in vain, for no brick is made.

Should you see a child crying for whatever reason. Know they are in pain and bless their heart. A BRICK IS MADE.

See you tears in the eyes of a man or woman. Know they are in pain or joy and bless their heart. A BRICK IS MADE.

See you someone who is in anger or rage. Know they are in pain for some reason and bless their heart. A BRICK IS MADE.

See you someone who is blind. They see not the wonders you do and bless their heart. A BRICK IS MADE.

See you someone who is deaf. They hear not the music of nature and bless their heart. A BRICK IS MADE.

See you someone who cannot speak. Their voice sings not the language you share and bless their heart. A BRICK IS MADE.

See you someone who is lame. They shuffle with

difficulty in the dance of life and bless their heart. A BRICK IS MADE.

See you someone who is disfigured. They are ugly only in the eyes that hold them so and bless their heart. A BRICK IS MADE.

See you someone who is poor. They know not the abundance that is theirs and bless their heart. A BRICK IS MADE.

See you someone who is hungry. They have forgotten how to feed them selves and bless their heart. A BRICK IS MADE.

See you someone who is naked or in rags. They know not how to clothe them selves and bless their heart. A BRICK IS MADE.

See you someone who is homeless. They have forgotten how to shelter them selves and bless their heart. A BRICK IS MADE.

See you someone who is a drunkard or an addict. What they take to numb their pain is now its cause and bless their heart. A BRICK IS MADE.

See you someone who is slow of wit. Their mind is in a cloud of darkness struggling to be free and bless their heart. A BRICK IS MADE.

See you someone who is a criminal. They have lost

their faith and bless their heart. A BRICK IS MADE.

See you someone who steals a childhood. They have had their childhood stolen and bless their heart. A BRICK IS MADE.

See you someone who takes a place before you. They take from you only that which has been taken from them bless their heart. A BRICK IS MADE.

See you someone who respects you not. They have no respect for them selves and bless their heart. A BRICK IS MADE.

See you someone who has taken a life. They know not what they have truly done and bless their heart. A BRICK IS MADE.

See you someone who is with disease. They know not that they could be well and bless their heart. A BRICK IS MADE.

See you someone who belittles others. They see them selves as unimportant and bless their heart. A BRICK IS MADE.

See you someone who robs others. They only rob bricks from them selves and bless their heart. A BRICK IS MADE.

See you someone who cheats others. They only

cheat them selves out of bricks and bless their heart. A BRICK IS MADE.

See you someone who hollers at others. They want to be heard but know not how and bless their heart. A BRICK IS MADE.

See you someone who lays a hand to others. They only strike bricks from their walls and bless their heart. A BRICK IS MADE.

See you a sick or injured animal. Bless its heart. A BRICK IS MADE.

See you any animal that has died. Bless its heart. A BRICK IS MADE.

See you the meat on your table. Know you that the animal gave up its life that you may be fed. Ask forgiveness and bless its heart. A BRICK IS MADE.

Let not a day go by that you have not given blessings. Open your heart to the world around you. Find in all things a reason to give blessings.

Your God has blessed you and all else. God's blessings come as easily as the rising and setting of the sun. Should not yours be given with the love you hold in your heart? Should you not bless all things around you that have been given to you? Think not that it makes no difference and it is but a small and unimportant thing to do. For I tell you truly, there is no blessing that you can give that is insignificant. Any blessing you give is a brick and will be given by God back to you unto the "nth" degree.

THE BOOK OF GIVING

That this leg may stand on solid ground and your giving begin, twice blessed are you who take this second leg to heart. That you may give to others, you must give to your self. Forgive your self all that keeps you from greatness. I am a child of God and from my soul I give. My heart beats to give to you, my God, and your children. I give myself the knowledge that I am made in God's image and likeness to be perfect, whole and complete. I am all I need to be to set the second leg as the foundation of God's will for me and all others.

The gift of giving is more than the mental process of I think I should, therefore I give. Be responsible in giving. If others benefit from your gift and you or your family are left wanting, this is not responsible giving, this is suffering. Be you abundant so others may prosper also. God has not meant for you to go hungry so others may eat. You are not to go naked so others may be clothed. You shall not live in the streets, that others may live in a mansion. There is no gift so small that it does not make a brick. But to give only so a brick is added to your mansion is done in vain, for no brick is made.

Be you loving to yourself as God loves you. A BRICK IS MADE. Give in return this love to all else around you. A BRICK IS MADE.

Be you kind to yourself that you may know kindness. A BRICK IS MADE. Give this kindness to all else around you. A BRICK IS MADE.

Be you your life's work for it is the cornerstone of life. A BRICK IS MADE. In return see that others have a life's work to be done. A BRICK IS MADE.

Be there food on your table so you will not go hungry. A BRICK IS MADE. Eat no more than you need to live so there will be food for others. A BRICK IS MADE.

Be you clothed so you will be protected from the heat or cold. A BRICK IS MADE. Give that which you do not use to those in rags. A BRICK IS MADE.

Be you sheltered so you will be dry and warm. A BRICK IS MADE. Make it so all have shelter.

A BRICK IS MADE.

Be you receiving when someone gives to you. A BRICK IS MADE. That others may receive from what you give. A BRICK IS MADE.

Be you filled in your basic requirements and that of your family. A BRICK IS MADE. See you then that others have the same. A BRICK IS MADE.

Be you relieved of your pain. A BRICK IS MADE. Give relief to those in pain. A BRICK IS MADE.

Be you sightful though you are blind. A BRICK IS MADE. Give you eyes to those who cannot see. A BRICK IS MADE.

Be you listening though you cannot hear. A BRICK IS MADE. Give you ears to those who cannot hear. A BRICK IS MADE.

Be you heard though you cannot speak. A BRICK IS MADE. Hear you those that cannot speak. A BRICK IS MADE.

Be active though you are lame. A BRICK IS MADE. Put those who cannot move into motion. A BRICK IS MADE.

Be you beautiful though you appear disfigured. A BRICK IS MADE. See beauty in those who seem to be ugly. A BRICK IS MADE.

Be you healthy though you are ill. A BRICK IS MADE. Give health to those who are sick. A BRICK IS MADE.

Be you seduced not to use drug or drink in ways for which it was not intended. A BRICK IS MADE. Give freedom to the enslavement of these, to those who are in its bondage. A BRICK IS MADE.

Be you quick in mind though you are slow. A BRICK IS MADE. Take time to understand those whose wit is dim. A BRICK IS MADE.

Be you honest though you have committed crimes. A BRICK IS MADE. Hold responsible ones who have committed a crime and then forgive them. A BRICK IS MADE.

Be you caring of a child's well-being though yours may have been taken. A BRICK IS MADE. See that others are caring of children and their well-being. A BRICK IS MADE.

Be you courteous to all and assume no place that is not yours. A BRICK IS MADE. Allow the elderly, the lame and children to go before you. A BRICK IS MADE.

Be you respectful though you may have been disrespected. A BRICK IS MADE. See that others respect one another. A BRICK IS MADE.

Be one who does not take a life. A BRICK IS MADE. Give mercy to and yet hold responsible one who has taken a life. A BRICK IS MADE.

Be you knowing that you are of greatness, though you may have been belittled. A BRICK IS MADE. Give in return greatness to those who have been belittled. A BRICK IS MADE.

Be you trustworthy taking not that which you have not been given or have not earned. A BRICK IS MADE. Give trust to others that they may be trustworthy. A BRICK IS MADE.

Be you soft-spoken with respect in your voice, though you may have been hollered on. A BRICK IS MADE. Require others to softly and with respect speak to each other. A BRICK IS MADE.

Be you gentle with your touch though you have been made to smart by a heavy hand. A BRICK IS MADE. See you that no one is laid a hand to. A BRICK IS MADE.

Be you so loving of an animal that you make room in your home for it. A BRICK IS MADE. Give sanctuary to animals in need. A BRICK IS

MADE.

Be caring of animals making them neither sick nor injured. A BRICK IS MADE. Give health to those animals in need of it. A BRICK IS MADE.

Be you fed by that which has not red blood. A BRICK IS MADE. Spare the life of an animal that you would otherwise use for food. A BRICK IS MADE.

Be you respectful of all life. A BRICK IS MADE. Take not so much that there is no more to come. A BRICK IS MADE.

Let not a day go by that you have not been giving. Open your mind to the world around you. Find in all life a reason and something to give. God gives life every second of every day. Should not you render with the same thoughts a life to be spared? Should you not think that all life is as precious as your own?

Think you not that it makes no difference or that any gift you give is insignificant. For I tell you truly, there is no gift you give too little that it will not be given back to you to the nth degree.

THE BOOK OF DEEDS

That this leg may stand on solid ground and

your deeds begin, thrice blessed are you who take this third leg to heart. You have blessed and you have given. Take that which needs to be done and do it your self. Say: "I am a child of God. My heart beats to do God's will for his children and me. This I can do, for God has made me perfect, whole and complete. I am made in God's own image and likeness. Therefore I am all I need to be and the works I do now anchor fast this leg."

The work that is done in your name is blessed. The work that is done by your name and your money is twice blessed. The work that is done by your hand is thrice blessed. When you see a need to be filled, you first feel it in your heart. Then you are moved emotionally with the desire to have it not be so. Your mind will search for a way to it otherwise. Then you take to task this need and with your hands you fill this need. There is no deed so small that it does not make a brick. Woe unto you who do this only so a brick is added to your mansion. This is done in vain, for no brick is made.

I, by my hand, end the pain of a child. THREE BRICKS ARE MADE.

I, by my hand, dry the eyes of a man or woman.

THREE BRICKS ARE MADE.

I, by my hand, soothe the anger and rage. THREE BRICKS ARE MADE.

I, by my hand, lead the blind through darkness. THREE BRICKS ARE MADE.

I, by my hand, speak the music of the deaf that they might hear. THREE BRICKS ARE MADE.

I, by my hand, hear the voice of the speechless that they may sing. THREE BRICKS ARE MADE.

I, by my hand, bind up the lame that they may travel their path and dance through life. THREE BRICKS ARE MADE.

I, by my hand, give comfort to the ill that they may have health. THREE BRICKS ARE MADE.

I, by my hand, open the eyes of all to see beauty, that none will shun away from the disfigured. THREE BRICKS ARE MADE.

I, by my hand, raise up the poor that they may make their own way and have abundant lives. THREE BRICKS ARE MADE.

I, by my hand, feed the hungry so they will learn to feed them selves. THREE BRICKS ARE MADE.

I, by my hand, dress the naked and those in rags with clean clothes, that they will clothe them selves. THREE BRICKS ARE MADE.

I, by my hand, build shelter with the homeless, that they will build shelter for them selves. THREE BRICKS ARE MADE.

I, by my hand, bring the tactility of love to replace the numbness in the drunkard or the addict, that they might feel the joy of life and release their pain. THREE BRICKS ARE MADE.

I, by my hand, remove the clouds of darkness, so the dim of wit will see they too have a place of importance. THREE BRICKS ARE MADE.

I, by my hand, hold those who commit a crime responsible to repay that which was taken, and they are forgiven that which is paid. THREE BRICKS ARE MADE.

I, by my hand, will make straight that which I have made crooked through mistake or knowledge, for I am honest. THREE BRICKS ARE MADE.

I, by my hand, give care and see to the well-being of children, that they may pass through childhood unmolested by word or action. THREE BRICKS ARE MADE.

I, by my hand, will make way for those who need a passage, be they young or old. THREE BRICKS ARE MADE.

I, by my hand, will not allow a life to be taken nor will I allow a life to be prolonged to suit my purpose. THREE BRICKS ARE MADE.

I, by my hand, will hold up to greatness those who have been belittled. THREE BRICKS ARE MADE.

I, by my hand, will not take the life of an animal nor will I prolong it to suit my purpose. THREE BRICKS ARE MADE.

I, by my hand, will open my house and heart to an animal. I will care for its needs and love it as if it were my child. THREE BRICKS ARE MADE.

I, by my hand, will only build that which does not destroy the sanctuary of animals in the wild. THREE BRICKS ARE MADE.

I, by my hand, will set my table with food that does not run red with blood. THREE BRICKS ARE MADE.

Let not a day pass that a deed has not been done. Open your arms to the world around you.

Find in all things a deed that you might do. God does for you more than you will ever know. Should you not do the same? Should not your deeds be given as freely?

Think you not that what you do makes little difference, or that it is an insignificant act. For I tell you truly no deed is so small that it will not be returned to you unto the nth degree.

Carry this book with you. When you know not what to do, it will guide you. As a builder's manual gives you the measurements of work to be done on the straight and level, so does this book give you measurements to live your life, that it may be straight and level. Go you now into the world and teach only love for God is with you all.

CHAPTER 3

12 POWERS OF A MASTERS

We possess few moments in our lives when we believe ourselves to be powerful. We may have moments when we *think* we can do just about anything, but those are few and far in between. Sometimes it seems like everything in our lives is going the way we feel it should. We are in the grove or the zone and we don't remember doing anything intentionally to have it all work out as wonderfully as it is. We wonder what we did or can do to make this happen in our lives. It continues to happen nonetheless, and we wonder why it can't be this way all the time. The truth is it can.

You can be the cause of things happening.

You are a child of God and as that child of God; you were given powers to assist you while you are here on Earth. Most of us don't know what these powers are, or how to use them. They remain available still the same, hidden and not in use. These little known attributes are built into our very nature and we don't even realize they exist.

Starting from the basics, we are human and we are fourfold in nature. We are physical, emotional, mental and spiritual beings. Each of these four natures holds powers that are accessible to each of us. When you know what these natures are and how to use them, you can begin to be proactive in your life. There are three powers for each of the four natures. They are called the twelve powers of a Master.

Below is an outline of the twelve powers of a Master; beginning with our lower natures:

PHYSICAL: MOTION OR ACTION

Emotional	LOVE
Mental	IMAGINATION
Spiritual	AWARENESS

EMOTIONAL: FEELINGS

Mental	CONCEIVE
Spiritual	FAITH
Physical	MANIFESTING

MENTAL: THOUGHT

Spiritual	PERCEPTION
Physical	STRENGTH of CHARACTER
Emotional	JOYFULNESS

SPIRITUAL: KNOWING

Mental	CREATION
Emotional	DESIRE
Physical	CONTRIBUTION

As humans, we are foremost concerned with the physical aspects of ourselves. This is where evidence of how we are doing in our lives shows up. However, all things originate in the spiritual realm and we must start the process of creating our reality and our lives from there. The physical realm is only the results of what we have already created with our attitudes in the spiritual realm.

When we begin to create something, out of a desire for something, usually we look around to see what we are producing in our lives. Then if what we are creating in our lives is not satisfactory, we think we need to do more. We begin to think, we should work harder or longer to produce what we want or need. If we remember along the way, we *may* ask for God's help, hoping God will hear us. More often then not, we come up with the same pattern of justification each time; we don't get the results we asked for... God must not want us to have it, or God didn't hear us. Oh, and yes, the best one of all... that we are unworthy to have it. We begin to believe we are undeserving and ultimately we stop trying altogether. The next time we want something for our loved ones, or ourselves we remember the times we asked God for help and the outcome of that request was a disappointment. We find it harder to believe that we can be successful in our manifestation, and in creeps that old pattern of beliefs.

What if we took another path to have these things? Another perspective? What if we took a quantum leap in the way we perceive ourselves as creators? From an entirely new standpoint, we can operate out of a totally new reality. We can be our own causal agent creating from the very source where all things are manifested.

Our spiritual selves are a part of that source. This is the highest aspect of our four natures. Within our spiritual selves are contained all of the other three aspects of our nature; the mental, the emotional and the physical. The spiritual realm is not just a big mystical place where only the spiritual stuff works. Pumping spiritual energy into a spiritual place is not only unnecessary but also impossible. First of all the spiritual self doesn't require anymore spiritual energy, it is already perfect. Secondly, the spiritual aspect of our selves is infinite in nature, constantly recreating itself in the process of constant manifestation. It is its own energy source.

When you send spiritual energy to the spiritual realm about something you want or need, what you are saying is, "Well here it is, I want it, I need it, so thank you very much!" We need to learn to use our spiritual selves as a beginning toward creating what we desire. In this process, we must learn to combine all of our other three natures toward our success. The relationships between our aspects and natures are all interlinked and operate synergistically. To be successful as your own creator, it is important to understand the interrelationships of all of the twelve gifts.

The Physical contains the physical-emotional, physical-mental and the physical-spiritual. This holds true for the other natures as well. In the Emotional there is the emotional-physical, emotional-mental and the emotional-spiritual. In the Mental are the mental-physical, mental-emotional and the mental-spiritual. Finally, we have the Spiritual, with the spiritual-physical, spiritual-emotional and the spiritual-mental. Each of these three sets of four is connected on different levels.

If you only concentrate in the physical level all you are doing is manipulating what is going on in the physical. A good example of this is trying to rearrange the deck furniture on the Titanic while it is sinking…in this example it is not being said your life is a shipwreck; take a look at what is physically happening here. If the ship is going down you can move all the furniture you want but you are not really affecting the fact that the ship is sinking. When you are working from only your physical nature, you are simply reacting to life, not changing any of the aspects that got you to that point.

On the other hand, when the focus is on the emotional, you are being run by your feelings. An event becomes all about how you feel about what is going on in the physical. Back to the Titanic example…you either feel happy because the band is still playing above deck, or unhappy because the dance floor has water all over it and you can't dance while the ship is sinking. In the emotional, the event is all about how you are feeling, and you want to feel good. Like in reaction to the physical, in the emotional your feelings are running your actions, not what the ship is doing.

The mental holds the same power over you. Your head is running the event and whatever you are thinking at the time, becomes the event. You get caught in cycles of trying to rationalize how it is happening, why it is happening and so on. You also think about what can be done to change what is happening. This is the most dangerous of the four natures as a focus or starting point because you can be in total denial of the true event. This happens in the mental process of our need to be right. The mental is run by the ego and it is lying to you. You could say you are a victim to your thoughts when you allow your mental self to guide you.

The last place you can live from is the spiritual. We tend to go to God or the spiritual in two ways. God is going to come and save the day, or it is Gods will. No matter which way you have been thinking, in the spiritual it came from a place of resignation. The event called the Titanic is happening and you are not participating in the event.

The above examples are extreme, but take a look at the ways each of the fourfold nature's effect not only your perception of an event, but your participation. Look to an event in your life and see if you can discern which of your four natures had become the event. You may even want to look at what is going on right now as you are reading this. Is one of your four natures primary to your experience in this moment? To break this pattern we need to change the way we approach the events in our lives. Instead of focusing on one nature and reacting, we can use the twelve powers of the Master for proactive involvement in each event.

Beginning with the spiritual realm, open your mind and connect with the creation process. The spiritual mental knows what is needed to create from nothing. From there move into the spiritual emotional which is the desire from which all things are created (this is not to be confused with want, meaning something needs to be filled not created). Desire is a spiritually proactive emotion that moves spiritual energy.

The next power to bring into play is the spiritual physical, or the vessel for creation to *become*. This shows up as a contribution of *action* from the spiritual realm because your spiritual nature is in alignment with the flow of spiritual energy.

Once you have established your spiritual connection, the next step is to engage the mental nature. The contribution from your three spiritual powers to the mental nature enters through your mental spiritual, opening your ability to perceive so that you can imagine what you are creating. Using your strength of character in the mental physical will focus the spiritual energy of creation into the mental emotional aspect of these three powers. When all of these aspects are working together, the result is joyful thinking.

As the three powers of the spiritual nature and the three powers of the mental nature enter the emotional nature in joy, they activate and incorporate the three powers within the emotional nature. Joy enters the emotional mental and brings about the emotional conception in the emotional spiritual feeling that the desire is done. This is known as faith, and from the fulfillment of faith, the emotional physical power will begin manifesting itself.

You have set in motion nine of the powers of a master. Nine is the number of completion. You are now ready to have the desire, manifesting through the three physical powers of a master. The physical emotional power is unconditional love through which the physical mental power is released so that your imagination is combining with the physical spiritual power of awareness. This in turn shatters the illusion that was created from your previous perceptions and allows the reality you are creating to come forward. This process is how you work as a *whole* being, using your whole self and all of your powers as tools toward manifesting anything and everything you desire.

Here is a crash course in how it all works. You are of the spirit and through the spirit you create your desires by contributing with your spiritual perceptions and the strength of your character. You conceive in faith to manifest out of awareness through love all that you can imagine. But it gets even better. If there is an event in your life that is not progressing as you desire, or the outcome is not what you intended, take a minute to sense which of your natures are not being used.

If your physical nature is not in touch, use the three powers of the physical in the emotional, mental and the spiritual to bring balance into what is missing.

If the problem lies within the manifesting of strength of character or in the contributions in the physical world, call in those powers, once again bringing in all of your powers for the success of your creative efforts.

If it is your emotional nature that you are not using, check to see if what you desire is consistent with love and joy.

Perhaps your mental nature is not cooperating. Ask yourself if you can imagine what it is you truly desire to create. Last of all be sure to check the spiritual aspects to see if you are using all of your spiritual powers.

These twelve powers are yours to use, but there is more to them then just getting the things you want. There is synchronization to all things, mechanical and biological, going on all the time. There is a self-fulfilling event taking place to bring about oneness that will happen in spite of our interference. Oneness that is consistent with all things.

This is how it works with a mechanical object as simple as a clock. If you have one hundred clocks with pendulums and start them all swinging randomly - all moving left, right, and having different positions within their arc. Leave them long enough and they will all begin to swing in perfect unison.

Another example from my own experience happened while I was working in an auto shop. I started a car and hooked up a timing light to check the timing of the engine. I set the light down so I could get the specifications for the model of the car. As I went for the book, I saw the guy next to me hooking up a timing light to his car. I went back to the car I was working on, picked up the light and noticed the other guy pointing his timing light back at me. We then had a timing light shoot out. I pulled the trigger and held it while the other guy did the same thing. Mine would fire with a burst of light and a second or so later, his would answer my light burst. Before we were able to get too involved in our timing light war, we were called away to help someone unload some heavy objects. We both went to help, letting our cars idle while we were gone. I don't know how long we were gone, but when we got back something strange had taken place. When he pulled his trigger and I pulled mine, I saw both cars were flashing at the same time. Here we have two different makes of cars, starting at different times, with lights flashing at different times, and now they were flashing at the same time.

On the biological side of this story comes another light account. While watching lightning bugs in the backyard with my daughter, they started to light up, as it got dark. I would point out one here, one there, and another across the yard. This went on for quite some time, as she is less then two years old and never before having seen a lightning bug. As we continued to watch them something astounding happened. All the lightning bugs started to light up at the same time, first there were three or four, then six or seven, and before long all of them were lighting up at the same time all over the yard.

A more complicated example is demonstrated with the involvement of people. I was attending a class called Inward Bound at which Alexander Everett was facilitating. The class was divided into ten groups of ten people each. Each group was then asked a question. We were told to come up with the best answer not the right answer. We were asked to discuss the question and prepare that answer. When the allotted time was up, Alexander Everett had one person from each group stand and give the groups answer.

Each person that spoke from each of the ten groups

gave the same answer! I knew in that circumstance we were all about something bigger then our opinions. The situation let us set ourselves aside, and as we did, we tapped into our twelve powers, working as one toward the same outcome!

When we use all of the powers we are given, which each of us carry within ourselves, this brings us to a state of wholeness - of oneness - from which to manifest. All of us are at the very thresh hold of creating a reality which we never realized existed. A reality in which we are working from our own oneness and creating from our own wholeness from within our own perfect set of powers. This Mastery exists within *you*. The question is do you dare change your perspective, taking your own power to create, to use it as the Master that you are?

CHAPTER 4

PRINCIPLES OF A MASTER

There is wisdom in each of the Principles of a Master. The thirteen Principles of a Master are set along spiritual lines to assist a Master in living a richer fuller life. They are also a set of actions that give the Master things to do in life. They are about each person living his or her own life fully, rather than being about who others are and trying to "fix" them. The beauty of this system is when you live your life by these principles, not only will your perception of reality be altered, reality it's self will be altered around you. This can also be expressed: "As a man thinkth so shall he be".

But why is this system called the Principles of a Master? Why not the rules, or the laws, or the guidelines? This question can be answered by remembering that when groups of people come together to successfully accomplish a goal, they have a plan to guide them. Masters are no different; however, in the beginning, everything was new, and methods had to be created as difficulties arose. Furthermore, the masters of that time didn't want rules or laws to abide by. Rules and laws were disregarded almost at once because people generally don't like to be told what to do. Rules and laws come from an outside source and are therefore easy to break. But when you break rules or laws, the consequence is usually some kind of trouble. There may be a physical consequence (like a speeding ticket) or an emotional consequence, (like the feeling of guilt caused by knowing you have done something bad); either way, while the person may "learn a lesson" and refrain from the inappropriate behavior for a time, eventually the behavior will reappear.

Principles, on the other hand, are incorporated into a person's being. You must "buy into" a rule before it becomes a principle. Principles are also much more general. "I will put others' needs before my own" is a broad statement about a way to act. "Don't cut in line," is a rule. It is almost as though principles are more forgiving. Because they become a part of a person's code of conduct, it is not possible for a person to "break" a principle unless he or she changes something fundamental.

When people want to function together as a group, the principles by which they live cannot be ignored. For the group to function smoothly, their "inner guidance systems" must be locked on the same general path and traveling in the same general direction. A group of Quakers searching for a solution to a territorial conflict would never include suicide bombing as a possible option, while a group of Islamic extremists might. In other words, the members of a group can more or less agree on basic principles or ways of being.

The questions we must ask ourselves now are: "What are the Principles we live our lives by now and how are they working for us? Are they working in our life such that we are happy and at peace. Do we go through life out of certainty or struggle?" It has been said that the real tragedy in life is that people will end up in the direction they are headed. The Principles of a Master allow an individual to grasp the possibility to change the direction.

- As a Master, I accept Gods love for me and know I am in Gods care.

- As a Master, I align my life with the spiritual Principles set forth in *The Book of Bricks.*

- As a Master, I honor and respect my gifts and the gifts of other Masters.

- As a Master, I teach only love.

- As a Master, I am ever vigilant of my traps and not the traps of other Masters.

- As a Master, I examine on a daily basis my participation with my gifts and traps.

- As a Master, I will be watchful for my selfishness and Ego.

- As a Master, I carry the message to all that would seek it.

- As a Master, I deny no one healing or teaching because of my feelings for or about him or her.

- As a Master, I receive fair compensation for teaching, healing and the work I create.

- As a Master, I render a 7th to wherever I receive spiritual nourishment or did profit from the work of another.

- As a Master, I set aside time to commune with God in prayer or meditation.

- As a Master, I am forever striving to grow as a person and a useful servant of God.

The First Principle: *As a Master, I accept God's love for me and know I am in God's care.*

(Some people are uncomfortable with the word, God. If this describes you, substitute "Supreme Being", "All Powerful Spirit", "Higher Power", or whatever name comforts you. Whatever you call this force, know it as benevolent power.)

Being able to accept God's love isn't easy for most people. As children we may have been told that God loves conditionally – we must attend the correct church, wear the correct clothing or head covering, we must think the correct thoughts, etc. By setting an unattainable goal, perfection of thought and action according to a set of arbitrary rules, and failing to achieve it, we come to the conclusion that we are unworthy. We may feel we need to earn love by being good enough to receive it.

But God gives love to us all, all the time, regardless of our level and expression of faith. We are in God's care and God only desires the best for us. Knowing this as a Master we can go about our lives in a state of peace rather than in a state of struggle. Accepting it allows us an opening to do our life's work instead of trying to be worthy out of some misguided thinking. We only waste our time and attention when we work to obtain God's love. Knowing we are in God's care frees us up to really go beyond where we ever thought we could. God is on our side, each and every one of us. With the promise of God's love as a guiding principle, is there anything we cannot do?

The Second Principle: *As a Master, I align my life with the spiritual Principles set forth in The Book of*

Bricks.

Many people find *The Book of Bricks* an easy to understand chapter. It is the foundation for all that has been given. Every time you read *The Book of Bricks* you will find something new that you missed the last time you read it. If you find yourself searching for an answer to a question or problem, you can find the solution in *The Book of Bricks*. And the more familiar you become with the books, the better you are prepared to deal with situations that perplexed you in the past. Everyone's journey through *The Book of Bricks* will be a little different. But it makes no difference if a person finds the path difficult or easy to follow, it is still a wonderful way to live one's life.

The Third Principle: *As a Master, I honor and respect my gifts and the gifts of other Masters.*

We are not all alike. Each person has natural talents – gifts – that set us apart from others. It is important to realize that those who do not understand a gift might not value it. Leaders, like those from the **Smyrna** church, are sometimes criticized for delegating and not doing for them selves. But the gift of those of Smyrna is leadership. Their motto could be expressed, "If it's to be, it's up to me; if it's to do, it's up to you." By leading, and delegating, they are living the third principle. If they were to insist on doing for them selves, they would be denying their precious gift of leadership.

Many times we find ourselves not understanding the gifts we have. This may result in taking a job that requires us to ignore our gifts to function. For example, those of the church of **Ephesus** whose gifts are uplifting others and helping them to find joy would be terribly mismatched with the job of corporate hatchet man. All day long they would be forced to deny their true nature and true gifts by downsizing and firing employees.

When we find we are working to support ourselves in a field that doesn't allow us to contribute out of our giftedness, we find ourselves being frustrated and unhappy. How many of us continue in a job, which slowly erodes our souls, only because it pays the bills? When we truly understand the gifts we have and the gifts we can be to others, we are able to contribute from this giftedness. Our work matches our inner natures and we can't help being successful and happy with our lives.

When we look to see another Master's gifts, we may not understand the way of them. We may be baffled by the ease someone else is able to accomplish what we cannot, or even feel upset because we can't do the same. It is especially easy to think the gifts of another get in our way when we try to attain what we assume we need. On the other hand, we may at times find our own gifts getting in the way of what we think we need or want. In both cases, what we forget is that we each have gifts according to our church. This is all part of the divine plan, and God has given something special and important to each of us. If we use the gifts we have, we can grow into the greatness we are to become. The bottom line is, we are all on a spiritual path. To hold the gifts of everyone with honor and respect allows each Master a way of passage.

The Fourth Principle: *As a Master, I teach only love.*

This should be the easiest principle of all, but it isn't. Teaching happens every time a Master takes action or speaks a word. What is taught should be a conscious decision of the Master. The goal should always be to strive to open a higher possibility. Masters must remember that they are changing reality through their words and actions.

It is a Master's choice to teach only love or not. Teaching only love brings about more love. We are all Masters, but we are all also human. There are times when events that happen in our lives can throw us off emotionally or obstruct our mental clarity, hampering the way we think. It is during these times of stress or sorrow that being a Master is most important.

Remembering the principle of teaching only love allows a person to do just that throughout life's bumps and bruises. The questions a Master needs to ask him or herself are, "Can I get my personal agenda out of the way? Can I, as a Master, be there for and about the teachings? Am I as a Master teaching love out of the giftedness I am? Have I used *The Book of Bricks* to get me clear so I can be about the work?" These questions can help you remember to teach only love.

The Fifth Principle: *As a Master, I am ever vigilant of my traps and not the traps of other Masters.*

All Masters have gifts and traps. We like to think gifts as good things and traps as bad things. It is, however, the traps that help us to grow spiritually. They are put there to force Masters to grow beyond where they are and what they think they can become.

Often it is easier to observe what someone else is doing or has done and conclude that they are caught in their traps. This game of analyzing others takes the focus off us. We feel superior when we see others floundering. But needing to be "right" is dangerous game to play where there can be no winner. When we find ourselves being drawn into controversy and arguments you can almost bet it has to do with traps.

There is a rule of thumb when it comes to traps that we can use if we find ourselves looking to see what traps another master is operating out of. We are probably operating from within our own traps and not our giftedness. A good test is to ask yourself if you have to justify what you are saying or doing. If so, you are working from the wrong side of the equation.

As we grow in spirit we become able to handle our traps. We come to terms with the fact a trap holds us back from living in our true giftedness. This is the reason we need to be vigilant about our own traps. The trick to a trap is really simple. It isn't so much about not getting into a trap. The real power over a trap lies in being aware of how your traps affect your thoughts, words and actions, and learning how to remove yourself from a trap by teaching only love.

The Sixth Principle: *As a Master, I examine on a daily basis my participation with my gifts and traps.*

This Principle is very important because it gives a Master a routine to follow at the end of the day, every day. When a Master follows this, it becomes much easier to live in their giftedness. In the time before sleep when a Master is alone with only their thoughts they can reflect on the day. Questions float to the surface and help the Master discover ways to improve.

What gifts were used to lift and empower others?

Did I spend this day as a force contributing to my family and my work; and did I touch the world in my giftedness?

Did I catch myself going to my traps during this day and was I able to stop myself before being trapped in them?

As I reflect this night, am I in a trap now and not aware of it?

Do I honor myself for the gifts I have and the traps I was able to avoid?

Before I sleep this night, can I truly say I gave it my best shot today?

There are times when any Master will fall short of their best shot. There is a great victory in being self-aware enough to know that we have fallen short. If we know this, we can do something about it. This nightly reflection will let the Master know if they have their gifts and traps under control, or if their gifts and traps have them under control.

The Seventh Principle: *As Master, I will be watch-*

ful for my selfishness and Ego.

This principle deals with worthiness issues. When a Master concentrates on having things, he or she is being selfish. When the Master concentrates on the unworthiness of others, he or she is taking an ego trip. Either way, the Master is taking rather than giving.

When we take more then we need, we are being selfish. When we bind people to us out of need, we are being selfish. When we put someone down to make ourselves look or feel better, this is ego. These are just sophisticated ways to take.

If we give only to get something back, we are takers. When we speak well of others only to make ourselves look good, we are takers. When we offer help to someone so that we have a hold on them, we are takers. When we need control, we are takers.

All of these behaviors, our petty selfishness and ego trips, exist because we feel unworthy. The truth is we are worthy as a child of God. We are all Masters and our needs are met. Taking begets more taking, but giving begets more being given too.

The Eighth Principle: *As a Master, I carry the message to all that would seek it.*

There is only one real message here. That is a message of love. The way we as Masters live by this principle is by following *The Books of Bricks* and teaching others that they are Masters also.

The Ninth Principle: *As a Master, I deny no one healing or teaching because of my feelings for or about him or her.*

Our prejudices are located deep within us. They are not easy to spot and not easy to change; the more obvious prejudices are those regarding race, religion, gender, and sexual orientation. These sometimes are more difficult to overcome than we realize. On another level, however, are the prejudices we hold the result from our ego and selfishness?

Is healing withheld from a person in need because we, in our infinite wisdom, have decided that we will not have any effect on the progress of the disease?

Do we sometimes not teach because we feel or think we are afraid we will look stupid or others will judge our sanity?

Will we not help or teach because of the judgments we have made about someone's ability or worthiness to receive our time and talents?

As Masters we must have only one feeling about

the person that stands before us: love for this person as child of God. Any other feeling a Master may have for someone, for whatever reason, must be set aside. The Master must be about the work at hand.

The Tenth Principle: *As a Master, I receive fair compensation for teaching, healing and the work I create.*

There is an exchange that takes place when someone compensates another for the work they have done. It is a form of energy that is exchanged. This exchange makes a way, so to speak, for energy to enter and to replace what was given, whether it is teachings or healing being given or received. To teach or heal for nothing is to say to another he or she is not worthy to receive. For a Master to ask for nothing the work they do or create is, in essence, to say either that the person receiving the gift is unworthy, or that the Master is not proficient enough to accept payment.

This Principle holds the power of worthiness in the hands of the Master. Most people want to pay for what they get. The tasks inherent in this Principle are to learn to accept payment for teachings and healings and to learn to ask for appropriate payment from each individual. Sometimes the beautiful smile of a person freed from pain for the first time in years is the same as the riches of kings.

The Eleventh Principle: *As a Master, I render a 7th to wherever I receive spiritual nourishment or did profit from the work of another.*

In order to keep the energy of giving and receiving open and moving, it is wise for you to give so that you may receive. To render a seventh to where you receive spiritual nourishment is a small price for feeding the spirit. Given that our spiritual knowledge doesn't generally come from organizations that have budgets, it is fitting to give to your mentors. This also means that Masters need to be open to receive from those to whom they give spiritual nourishment. The Master who teaches the work of another and is paid for it, in turn needs to give a seventh back to the source. In the spirit of this Principle, also include giving credit to the one from whom you received information.

The Twelfth Principle: *As a Master, I set aside time to commune with God in prayer or meditation.*

We are busy people; supporting ourselves and our families, in addition to the spiritual work we are doing. We may find there is little time for much else. Sometimes we feel like the woodsman who didn't have the time to sharpen his ax because he was to busy cutting trees. His work became harder and harder as his ax became duller and duller.

When we take the time to sit down and sharpen our spiritual ax, our work becomes easier. By making time to meditate, we become clearer on the work we are doing and make fewer mistakes. We are also more loving and kind. We find ourselves becoming ill less often, if at all. Nourishing our bodies and spirits helps us maintain our own balance.

The Thirteenth Principle: *As a Master, I am forever striving to grow as a person and a useful servant of God.*

We are in this world to grow physically, mentally, emotionally and of course spiritually. These four aspects are what make us the people we are. Developing and maturing in each aspect gives us the balance necessary for further growth. As we grow in these ways, we are better able to serve in the divine plan of love. One of the big mistakes made is when we arrive at a point in our lives and we are done.

These Principles are given to help the Master grow not to dictate a code of conduct. I know for me I have not always been able to follow **them to the letter of** what is written and I don't **believe this is their pur-**pose. If we lock ourselves into the letter of the law, we have missed their greater importance: us. I am sure that when Michael gave these he was more about the spirit of the principles. I know we can argue what the letter of the law of these principles is saying, but not the spirit of them.

CHAPTER 5

KEYS OF A MASTER

SEVEN KEYS TO THE KINGDOM OF GOD

"When your kind masters the use of them all it will truly be a heaven on your earth. I say unto you now, long have you not used them. Yet though lost, they have been with you all the time. I call them forth that you will know them. I speak as I am for I am as you as are we all as is all." —*Shekinah*

Your kind has come to believe you are unworthy of it. You have lost the ability to truly love your self as the child of God you are. You cannot love one another as you did before you came here. These first two will make the way for this again. I give you the keys, yet it is you that will have to learn to use them. — *Shekinah*

1. LOVE YOUR SELF AS GOD LOVES YOU.

Love your self without hesitation or reservation as God loves you. Unconditional as due to the child of

God you are. Because you are.

2. LOVE OTHERS AS YOU WOULD LOVE GOD.

To love others as you would love God, is loving God. For I ask you what parent does not want their child loved more then they? Is there one of God's children to be loved less? Did not Jesus teach this?

3. HONOR AND LOVE THIS WORLD THAT YOU LIVE AS THE HOUSE OF GOD.

Your kind has come to believe you were given dominion over the earth and all living things. Yet this is not what was given. Your kind was given charge of the garden. You were to care and keep it. Long has it been forgotten the gift of the garden and all it would profit. As wanton children humankind has forgotten the garden is for all. The animals that were given sanctuary there have been cast out. The harmony of the garden is all but lost. I give you the third key that you may return to the garden.

4. CARE FOR THE WELL BEING OF EACH OTHER.

As I see it, this key means more then just caring about others. To me it means to be proactive in the well being of others. If I have to do with a little less so that someone else can have what he or she needs, I act on it. I am responsible that others are respected. I do not do damage to ones name or the work they do.

5. AS A CHILD OF GOD I HAVE THE RIGHT TO COMMUNE WITH GOD AS THE TEMPLE OF THE I AM.

This key opens up the truth that we can commune with God all on our own. We don't need to have anyone talk to God for us. Given we are all made by God in Gods image and likeness; we are in fact temples of God.

6. I DO NOTHING. THE LIGHT OF I AM ALLOWS EVERYTHING. AS I BEHAVE LIKE THE LIGHT ALL THINGS ARE POSSIBLE.

When we can let go of our illusion of being in or able to control everything and everyone around us we begin to act as the light. For us allowing things to happen out of love opens the possibility for our desire to be manifested. When we seek control of others in the things we desire we close down possibilities. Events that may seem to be getting in the way may only be a set of circumstances to quicken the path to have our desires achieved. God is love; desiring for us all the wonderful things in life. God allowed all by saying let there be, as children when we do the same we can create the same.

7. We have yet to receive the seventh and final key.

CHAPTER 6

ONENESS OF A MASTER

In the beginning there was one. This one was God and from God came everything and everything was God. There was oneness with all that was created. We could say this oneness ended with the fall of man. Man gave up this oneness for knowledge and lost the awareness of the oneness with God. In time man lost the knowledge that he was aware of the oneness. Man became separate from God, from other men, and from all that was created. Man became unto himself and was lost. As each generation was born, there was more and more separation taking man further from God, from other men and from all creation.

But the separation has left a gaping hole in human existence. We find ourselves looking for that perfect love our spirit knows exists. Some fill this void with drugs, alcohol or sex. Others look in organized religion, work, academics or sports. Still more expect to find the missing piece in relationships and families. Fruitless searching for this love in the physical realm, emotional realm, and the mental realm, has given us the illusion that the deep spiritual love we seek is outside us and outside our abilities.

The "we" and "us" ("us" being another form of "we") of this hypothesis are inclusive pronouns meaning more than just one person. "We" becomes more powerful as numbers increase. The more "we's" there are, the greater the illusion of power we have. We believe we can control more of what goes on around us in our world and our lives. "Our" adds possession to the power of "we". "We", "us" and "our" are collective terms—meaning many beings with the same thought or purpose. "We" become a group, and the group has a sense of synergy or of singleness of purpose in acting as one. So ingrained is this into our thinking, the brain cannot readily access oneness in understanding without these terms.

The illusion is that the larger the group of like-minded people there is, the closer to oneness we all become. We believe that when enough of us come together we can achieve oneness. We know intuitively that our purpose can convert others from being "them" to being "us". Then we will have oneness!

That sounds really great—getting a critical mass of "us" to become one and cause change. But there is a problem. By the very nature of "we", "us" and "our", there is separation so cunning and insidious "oneness" can never happen.

"They", "them", "those", "their" and of course "you" are outside the realm of "us", "we" and "our". Everything that denotes something outside is in separation from the "we". "They" make the laws; "they" cause the problems. These others, the "they" of the equation, have become the antagonists of our purpose by the very fact they are separate from the "we". "He" and "she" also put someone out of the realm of oneness as easily as "they" or "them" or their grouping is outside of "us". "He" did that or said that, or "she" did that or said that, and "they" did or said that. When "you" did or said, it becomes the same separation.

The illusion of "us" and "them" gives us the promise that "we" can attain oneness. Our goal is just beyond our grasp and "we" are so close "we" can almost touch it. All "we" need is a few more like "us" to make it happen, to bring about the critical mass for everything to change. There in itself lies the problem. The truth is the words "we", "us" and "our", are the big lie that keeps the separation in motion. The truth is, there is no "us", "we", or "our" in oneness. Each word expresses an idea that purposefully sets others outside "me". When using these words, people tend to think of the inclusive nature of the language, but the words are exclusive by nature. No "one" is in oneness regardless of the number of people who are of the same thought or purpose. "We are one" is a great and wonderful concept, but it just isn't so. There is no oneness past "I am". "I am" is all there is.

Here is a higher possibility that can really effect a change. Agree, for a moment, that the definition of "concept" is "a perception or an idea that is understandable" and a "context" is defined as "an environment or framework that allows for being". Now imagine – "What if "we", "us" or "our", were not used to tie a concept together? What if no concepts were to be used at all? What if there is only context to become?"

Ideas can be understood in varying degrees depending upon analytical skills of a person. In scientific inquiry, for example, a hypothesis is made and evidence is gathered to test the hypothesis. This process "proves" the hypothesis. The greater a personal ability to analyze the data gathered, the greater the person's understanding of the meaning and applications of the hypothesis. This is a great procedure for observable phenomenon of the natural world. But oneness is not observable in the real world—it can only be manipulated as an idea.

On the other hand, context, an atmosphere that allows for being, enables humans to define and experience oneness. What is the context? The context is "I". Not the separation of "we" or "us" or "our", not even "they", "them", "their" or for that matter "you". "I" is all there is. "We" cannot, but "I" can. "You" are really "I", as are "us" and all the rest of the terms under discussion. In order to bring about a true shift in the consciousness of the world, we need to stop being "us" and become "I".

This is not simply a discussion of words but an attempt to awaken the reader to the awareness of oneness. Be careful. The first step is the awareness of knowing something is there. That something is separation – all those pronouns in the first part of this chapter. But the next step is a bit more tricky.

Oneness isn't something a person understands on an intellectual level. Oneness is a readiness, an openness, a beginning and ending all wrapped up into one. Take, for example, free will. Each person has been given free will to make choices. As soon as you exercise your free will in choosing you have closed the possibility for the context of oneness. There is no free will in oneness because there is no need for free will. All choices are always possible. Oneness doesn't mean a person has to get rid of everyone else for there to be only one. It means that everyone is included as "the one".

For the sake of argument let's say I am going to teach a class. It works like this:

I get the material ready for the class and go to the place where the class is going to be held. I set everything up and when the students arrive I begin teaching the class. I start talking to the students and if I have prepared properly the students understand the flow of the class. From time to time a student will ask a question. I need to answer so that the student gets their question answered. Some of the students may want to argue a point with me about something I said. We exchange thoughts and the point is settled. By the end of the class everyone has learned something and we are all in a higher place of understanding. Class over.

This sounds simple but now let's look at it coming from oneness rather then the student/teacher relationship of separateness. I am going to teach a class. It works like this:

I get the material ready for what I am teaching and go to the place where the class is going to be held. I set everything up and when I arrive I begin teaching the class. I start talking to "me" and if "I" have prepared properly the "I" understands the flow of the class. From time to time "I" will ask a question and "I" need to answer so "I" get my question answered. "I" may want to argue a point with "me" about something "I" said. "I" exchange thoughts and "my" point is settled. By the end of the class "I" have learned something and "I" am in a higher place of understanding. Class over.

The point is "I" am really teaching "me", because oneness shows up at any given moment in time and at every given moment in time. Whether the room is full of people or there is just a few "I" am only teaching one and that one is "I". When "I" go to a class where someone else is teaching, "I" am really going to "my" class and "I" am teaching me.

Robert Heinlein, in *Stranger in a Strange Land*, wrote that his main character "groked" people, situations and ideas. To grok something is to partake of it, to eat it, so that it becomes part of the individual on a cellular level. At this level, it is not necessary to explain with words – things are understood to a depth that words would impede the understanding.

To borrow this context from Heinlein, if you "grok" this chapter without needing to explain it, you are now in the "I". This is not something "you" can understand as "you". Nor is it possible to observe as a phenomenon taking place in the moment. It is not a quantum event to which "you" are a party. It *is* the oneness of all things being at the same place and in the same moment. It is the oneness of a Master being only one. Ask yourself in this very moment.

WHAT AM I PRETENDING NOT TO KNOW?

CHAPTER 7

A MASTER'S STORY

There was a young boy who wanted to be a Master. He lived in a small town but just knew in his heart there was more to his life. He knew he was put on this Earth to make a difference. True, he was loved by his mother and father and had friends, but he felt there was something missing.

One day he came up with an idea. If he could learn to be a Master, he could do something important with his life. That very same day he left his town and went in search of a Master from whom he could learn. As he traveled down the road the days turned to weeks and the weeks turned into months. Finally, he came upon a group of people on the side of the road. There must have been over two hundred people sitting around, listening to a teacher. The boy asked one of the people close to the road, "Who is that man teaching out in the field?" He was told it was Master Jones, a very kind and loving person filled with inner knowing and wisdom.

The boy jiggled on the balls of his feet in anticipation. He knew this Master could tell him the secret to being a Master himself. The Master looked up and saw the boy standing at the edge of the crowd. Realizing that he hadn't seen this boy before, the Master called the boy to come up and talk with him. The young boy went up to the Master.

"What do you want?" the Master asked.

"I want to be a Master. I only need one thing. I need the true secret that will make me a Master. Will you teach that secret to me?"

The old Master looked deeply into the boy's eyes as if trying to peer into his soul. "Come back at first light tomorrow, and I will tell you this great secret," he finally said.

It was impossible to sleep that night. The boy tossed and turned on the bed of hay a friendly farmer had fixed for him. Long before first light, the boy was on his feet and traveling back along the road to the place where he had met the Master.

Finally, the time came and the young boy was standing in front of the old Master. "Are you sure you want to know the secret of being a Master?"

"Yes, very much, with all my heart," the boy said breathlessly.

With this the old Master leaned forward and whispered in the boy's ear. The boy's grin stretched wide.

Now he knew the secret.

The boy returned to his small town. At first, things seemed different; but, as time went on, he fell back to the way his life had always been. He didn't really think he was making a difference. After a time, he began to wonder if something was wrong with him. But he discarded that thought. After all, the old Master had looked into his eyes and judged that he was worthy to be a Master.

But if he wasn't the problem, what was? Perhaps the old Master really wasn't an important enough Master to really know the secret, he finally concluded. Before long the boy, no longer young, was off again down the road to find a more important Master who *really* knew the secret. On his journey he passed Master Jones sitting in the field teaching a huge crowd of people. He waved to the old Master as he passed. "Nice old man," he thought, "too bad he didn't really know the secret of being a Master."

After two weeks of difficult travel the boy came upon what looked like a small town. When he asked the name of the town, he was told it wasn't a town at all. It was the place where Master Bob lived, and all the thousands of people were here to learn from him. The boy's heart jumped for joy. He knew for certain this had to be an important enough Master to really know the secret.

Scanning the crowd, the boy located a man who might be a student of Master Bob. Approaching him, he asked, "Can you help me?"

"Perhaps," the man answered.

"I need to see Master Bob."

"He's right there," the man gestured.

"No, I need to speak with him."

"Oh," the man said mildly, and set off at a brisk pace, weaving his way through the throng, the boy hurrying after him. They worked their way through the crowd, finally arriving in front of the Master.

"Master Bob," the man called, "this young man would like to speak with you."

Master Bob turned and looked deeply into the boy's eyes before answering. "Yes. How may I help you?" Master Bob asked.

"I know I am supposed to do something important in my life. Or maybe with my life. But I can't until I know the secret of being a great Master. Can you tell me the secret?"

Master Bob looked at him carefully, then replied, "See me at first light tomorrow and I will tell you the secret of being a Master."

"Oh, thank you," the boy said and turn to go. As he left, he smiled broadly. He was too excited to sit still, so he spent the rest of the day walking around the grounds listening to the students talk to one another.

He had never heard such wonderful things being said. He took his evening meal with other students as the sun was setting on its way to end a perfect day. The boy was given a blanket and a place to sleep, however he wanted to sleep outside under the stars. Spreading his blanket on the ground, he sat down, looked up and thought, "Finally, I will learn the *real* secret". It took a long time before the young boy drifted off to sleep.

The next morning before the sun came over the horizon the boy woke. Just as soon as he recognized where he was, his mind started racing. He went to the river to wash quickly before meeting with Master Bob. He wanted to look his very best because today was a very special day, the day he would learn the secret.

The boy rushed over to the building where Master Bob sat and met with his students and talked to visitors. He was early, and he knew it, but he just wanted to be close to the Master who was about to give him the greatest gift in the world. The boy sat there for hours thinking of all he would do when he received the secret. His thoughts were interrupted by the student he met the day before who was to take him to see the Master. Nervously he got to his feet and followed the student in to see Master Bob.

Eyes closed, Master Bob was sitting on pillows upon a raised platform so everyone could see him from where they sat. As the young boy was led down the aisle he could see there were incense sticks burning around Master Bob. When the student and the boy came to where Master Bob was sitting, Master Bob opened his eyes.

"You are the boy that wants to know the secret to being a Master," he said.

"Yes," the boy responded. "You told me if I came back this morning you would tell it to me."

"So I did," the Master said. "Come closer and I will whisper it in your ear." The boy almost shaking out of his sandals leaned close to the Master.

The Master looked into the boy's eyes and drew back from the boy.

"Is something wrong?" the boy asked.

"No," said Master Bob. "I just want you to tell me something first."

The boy said, "Anything. I will tell you anything you want to know."

"I was wondering if you had ever been told this secret before."

"Well," the boy answered. "I did ask Master Jones, but he wasn't a very important Master like you are Master Bob. He only had a few hundred people around him. He does his teaching outside, not in a beautiful building like you have. Master Jones was a very kind man but he didn't have anything like this, so

I figured he probably didn't know that much."

"Oh, I see," said Master Bob. Turning to one of the people that worked in the house, Master Bob asked, "Do we have anything for this boy to do?"

"We are in need of a stable boy," a student mentioned.

"Yes," the boy said, "I could do that."

"Very well," said Master Bob. "You are going to clean the stables, and when I call for you, I will tell you what you want to know."

"Ok," said the boy. "When you call for me, you will tell me. But for now, I will clean the stables."

"Yes," said Master Bob.

The days, then the weeks, months and years drug by slowly. The boy spent every day cleaning the stables. He sent all the animals outside and removed the waste they left from the night before. He removed the soiled straw and replaced it with fresh, clean straw. He swept the floor and washed it every day. Fresh food and water were measured according to the need of each animal. As he grew older he did his work more quickly, but never without excellence.

Finally, near the end of the tenth year, a student came to the stables. "Master Bob sends you greetings and asks if you would favor him with your presence tomorrow at first light." The boy, now a grown man, was speechless, and could only nod his "Yes".

The years fell away quickly. It felt just like the very first time that he had come to see the Master. He could hardly sleep that night but washed carefully, removing the muck from the stables. He went up to the Master before first light and waited to be called to speak with him.

Master Bob came down from his platform and out of his chamber. He leaned over and whispered in the young man's ear. The young man jerked upright upon hearing what Master Bob told him. He stood still, his expression of confusion slowly turning to one of anger.

"I would have thought you would have been happy to hear the secret. Why are you upset?" asked Master Bob.

"I worked for 10 years, only to hear the same words Master Jones told me when I was young!" the young man exploded.

Master Bob looked at the young man and said, "Now do you believe?"

The point here is simple. You have the secret, and you can do something to make a difference in the world. It matters very little where you get the secret because you are a child of God. You are made in God's own image and likeness. You are perfect, whole and complete just the way you are. You can choose to go from here and make the difference. Or you can doubt that you learned anything or anything happened for you. Remember there are plenty of Masters in the world that will let you clean their stables to earn what you have already learned. It is up to you.

CHAPTER 8

A MASTER'S WORDS OF POWER

I have come to find over the past years, there are only two places a Master can stand, forgiveness and apology. From these places come what I call the Master's words of power. Again I say this is not *the* truth, *the* light or *the* way. I can only speak for myself. I can only tell you about the changes that have taken place for me, and the difference these words have made for people that have heard them and have taken them to heart.

Everyone brings a unique set of life events along, whenever and wherever we go. These life events have accumulated from the day we were born till present day, and will continue to accumulate until life ends. These events have combined with luck from the genetic draw to make us the people we are today. Some events have been good and others have been not so good.

From this huge bin of life experiences we have chosen, thoughtfully or randomly, certain events in which we pay more attention. These are the experiences by which we have chosen to live our lives. Not only have we chosen certain events to emphasize, we have rewritten the history around these events to support the kind of person we perceive ourselves to be. We have made up things about each event, and from that point the latest version becomes the truth. John Hanley said, "We are that we interpret and the moment we interpret we become our interruptions."

If this is true, what have we become from the interruptions of the events in our lives? What has happened to us along the way? What have we caused to happen to others? Must we be stuck in our past events, living and reliving life through this dim and cloudy mirror?

There is a way out of the past and into the moment of now. The first is an apology to you that you can give to others. The second is forgiveness you can give to others that you may forgive yourself.

THE APOLOGY FOR YOU

I want to tell you I am sorry. Not because I did something to you, or I am trying to get off the hook for something. I am sorry that as a child your innocence was used against you. I am sorry for all the times you wanted to share your words of wisdom and you were told to shut up. I am sorry for the genius you possessed in the ideas you gave, and you were told that you were stupid. I am sorry for the times you did your very best and were told it wasn't good enough. I am sorry for the times you were made fun of because you were different in some way. I am also sorry that your feelings were hurt and no one was there to comfort you. I am sorry for the tears you cried with pain and no one was there to wipe them. I am sorry that you gave your heart like a precious present, and it was refused. I am sorry for the times you were hurt whether justly or unjustly, and for the times you were alone and afraid with no one there for you. I am sorry for all promises made to you that were broken. I am sorry for the wishes you made that were not fulfilled and your dreams that were shattered. I am sorry for the times you were helpless and at the mercy of others, finding there was none. I am sorry for the times in your life that you felt like you didn't matter. I am truly sorry for the times you felt that even God found you unworthy of love. Someone owes you an apology just for these events of your life. . . . I am so, so sorry.

You are a child of God that is perfect, whole and complete. You are a magnificent human being and deserving of love and happiness. Your happiness is not mine to give; but, if it were, I would give it. Loving you is easy. I love you just the way you are, and I really don't want anything from you. Bless your heart, and teach only love.

FORGIVENESS

I forgive you for the times you would not listen to what I had to say. I forgive you for ignoring me when I needed you. I forgive you for the times you yelled at me for things I did not do. I forgive you for the times you lied to me or about me. I forgive you for the times you wouldn't let me just be a child and play. I forgive you for the times you pushed me out of your way. I forgive you for all the times you laid a hand to me whether I deserved it or not. I forgive you for abusing me physically or mentally. I forgive you for not being there to dry my tears or ease my pain when I hurt. I forgive you for belittling me and making me feel small. I forgive you for the promises you broke to me. I forgive you for stealing from me. I forgive you for slanderous words you said about me. I forgive you for breaking my heart that I gave as a gift to you. I forgive you for betraying my trust and me. I forgive you for cheating me. I forgive you for holding hostage the things I loved so that you could get your way. I forgive you of all these things and all those things I don't know that I should forgive you for. Bless your heart. I can do no other but forgive. For I know that in this forgiveness I give to you I make the way for my own forgiveness of me. I do not seek your, or any other's forgiveness in this. I seek to forgive myself for the things I have done and the pain I have caused others to suffer.

For I am a child of God, I am made in God's own image and likeness. I am perfect, whole and complete. I need to act accordingly.

AFTER WORD

"Write that which I give you for they are the highest of teachings. Give them to those of your kind that they may grow in spirit. The words of my book will bind themselves to the soul of human kind if not the mind. Our kind offers yours wisdom that you may make your selves a new and that of the world you live a paradise. As the Book of Knowledge was given to Enoch from Ratziel, I give you the Book of Wisdom that your kind may be wise in that which they know. These writings are as the charts for a ship set at sea. Use them as they are given and they will navigate you through the most troubled of waters. I tell you truly your will to use these wisdoms are yours and yours alone."

—*Archangel Gabriel*

If you have reached this point in your reading you have received the wisdom to live your life the way you were meant, as a child of God. These teachings are the foundation and cornerstones of all spiritual teachings.

You may not have understood everything in this book and that is all right. Each time you read it you will find more and more wisdom coming to life for you. As you "the person" connects with you "the spirit" your mental, physical, emotional and spiritual will begin to work as one. This oneness will allow you to become more effective in all areas of your life. As you incorporate these teachings you will find greater peace and harmony with others. I wish you happiness on your journey called life. Be at peace and teach only love.

— *Joseph Crane*

DR. JOSEPH CRANE. DD. PHD.

Author of *"Teaching the Masters"* and *"Blessings, Gifts, and Deeds"*, along with being co-author of *"On the Wings of Heaven"*

Joseph Crane is a Viet Nam veteran. During his service in the Navy, Joe and other crewmembers were saved by an unseen voice that directed them to safety during a friendly-fire explosion aboard an aircraft carrier. This voice continued to call out his name at different times throughout his life until a being of light came forward in a form that Joe could see, and even touch.... a very tall and powerful angel.

For the past eight years Joseph has demonstrated his commitment to share the messages from the angelic realm. These messages contain information about healing using frequencies, spiritual revelations, and becoming the Master we all are. The healing tools given include sacred oils, frequencies to assist the removal of cancer and pain, and The Gate of Grace. This gate acts as a gateway between the angelic realm and our own. It is used for angelic communication and for healing. Joseph created the healing modality

AcuTuning. This modality uses tuning forks tuned to certain frequencies the same as the meridian points and sacred oils from the angelic realm to achieve similar results as acupuncture. All of these tools assist us in healing physically, emotionally, and mentally. Joseph has assisted many others in healing and has seen many miracles take place over the past four years.

Joe Crane tells the story of the angelic encounters that are now a part of his life in his books. These angelic encounters have had a profound effect on many people. The information and messages imparted by the angels are quite profound and directed to us all. The angel charged Joe to find seven masters and teach them to teach. He did this and now the message has spread to more then 500 in what the angel called gatherings.

In these few years Crane has demonstrated his commitment to sharing the messages from the angels he sees, one of which is the Archangel Michael. Joe Crane's lectures are filled with challenging concepts and the warmth of his down-to-earth humor. Joseph's considerable experiences as a workshop trainer and group leader enable him to connect deeply and authentically with his audiences. Joseph holds a Doctorate in Divinity and a PhD in Religion.

Joe's lectures and workshops contain many of the angelic messages. The following are just a few of the topics he presents across the country.

- The Seven Gifts of Humanity and the Well of Souls
- *The Book of Bricks* and how to build one's Spiritual Mansion
- Decoding the Book of Revelation.... A Past, A Present, and A Promise
- The Twelve Powers of a Master
- Obtaining Oneness
- Healing Principles and Tools given from the Angelic Realm
- The 50 Gates of Ascension

Crane is not a channeler, a psychic, or a medium. He's an everyday guy put into an extraordinary situation. The angel that started appearing to him eight years ago continues to appear bringing even more incredible information for humanity than before. And to top things off, this angel appears in 3D, physical form. Joe can touch the angel and the angel has physically touched Joe. They have conversations like you would with your best friend.

Joe Crane is also available for guest speaking, lectures and seminars in your area where he shares on the teachings from the angelic realm and the writings from his books. He currently resides with his family in the Texas Hill Country.

Give the Gift of Love: *Teaching the Masters: The Instruction Book God Forgot to give you*
Check your Local Bookstore or Order Here

__ **YES,** I want ___ copies of *Teaching the Masters: The Instruction Book God Forgot to give you* for $14.95 each.

__ **YES,** I would like ___ 2 ml bottle(s) of the *Michael's oil* spoken of by the editor for $30.00 each.

__ **YES,** I am interested in having Dr. Joseph Crane speak or give a seminar to my company, association, school, or organization. Please send me some information.

Include $3.95 for shipping and handling for one book or oil, and $1.95 for each additional book or oil. Texas residents must include applicable sales tax. Canadian orders must include payment in US funds, with a 7% GST added. Payment must accompany orders.
Please allow 3 weeks for delivery.

My check or money order for $_____ is enclosed.

Please charge my ___Visa ____MasterCard ____ American Express ___Discover

(continues overleaf)

121

Name_____

Organization_____

Address_____

City/State/Zip

_____

Phone _____

E-mail _____

Card # _____

Exp. Date _____

Signature _____

Call (830) 751-2412
Make your check payable and return to
Angel Gate Creations
501 Joel Lane
Lakehills, TX 78063

www.teachonlylove.com
Fax: (830) 751-2412